Behind the Curtain: Ideology and Neoliberalism

Alan McGuire

Table of Contents

For Conchita

Images all used under Creative Commons

Gramsci Image from Wiki Commons

Che image from Wiki Commons

Soccer drawing by Pearson Scott Foresman via Wiki Commons

Lenin image from Wiki Commons

G20 Meltdown protest in London on 1 April 2009 by Jonny White, CC BY 2.0 <https://creativecommons.org/licenses/by/2.0>, via Wikimedia Commons

Image of Margaret Thatcher by Rob Bogaerts, CC0, via Wiki Commons

Presidente Allende by Original by Post of the Soviet Union, SVG by Merlin2525, CC0, via Wikimedia Commons

Editorial cartoon depicting Charles Darwin as an ape (1871) published in The Hornet, a satirical magazine via Wiki Commons

President Bill Clinton greets British Prime Minister Tony Blair following his arrival to Belfast.1998 Barbara Kinney White House Photograph Office via Wiki Commons

Aladdin find the lamp by Felix Octavius Carr Darley (1821-1888), Public domain, via Wikimedia Commons

France in 2000 year (XXI century). Building Site. Villemard, Public domain, via Wikimedia Commons

Mark Fisher at the Barcelona Museum of Contemporary Art in 2011 by MACBA, CC BY-SA 2.0 <https://creativecommons.org/licenses/by-sa/2.0>, via Wikimedia Commons

Introduction

"Ideologies have no heart of their own. They're the whores and angels of our striving selves." John Le Carre

The main idea of this book is to equip the reader with an understanding of ideology from a Marxist point of view. When we hear the word ideology it is often used to discredit people as being politically motivated, with their heads in the sky. They don't live on the real world like the rest of us, they don't speak common sense. Sometimes this can be true, but most of the time it is a way of discrediting an alternative. An alternative that threatens the wealth and power of the rich.

Trasfondo is a Spanish word that is simply translated into 'background'. But not all translations are direct copies: trasfondo has an added meaning which is the subtext of the context. The underlying meaning behind what is in front of us. This is ideology.

We have successfully been sold the idea that there is no alternative to capitalism: the famous Margaret Thatcher line. That, and our current version of capitalism without limits, neoliberalism, is the best form to allow people to get rich based on their individual mindsets and attributes. As I hope to prove in this book, it is far from the truth.

I wrote the original version of this book during the 2019 Coronavirus pandemic. I think the timing of this is not coincidental. During times of great crisis, like war, famine and pandemics, we see the old ideas come to be tested.

If you work hard, you can achieve anything. Then why aren't they giving the nurses, doctors, cleaners and teachers pay rises?

People don't want to work anymore. Says the influencer on her second trip to Dubai this year. Where did she get the money to invest in her business again?

The market always delivers. How much was wasted on failed schemes during the pandemic? Was it the public NHS or the corporate companies that saved our asses?

We can't afford the migrants and the unemployed on benefits forever. But we can subsidise people going out for meals in private restaurants, to pay 80% of the nation's wages and throw away millions to the private sector to compensate for their losses.

Most of the rhetoric that came with the 80s/90s version of yuppie neoliberal capitalism is starting to show its age in the 2020s.

In short, ideas matter. They are used to justify the tightening of borders to refugees whose homes we have helped destabilise, they are used to justify not building public housing, or investing in public services, ideas are used to persecute the working class, migrants, the LGBTQ community, the disabled and women.

Neoliberalism is a big scam to justify obscene inequality in the world. Ideas are used to keep the rich and powerful on top and turn us against each other. The likes of Jordan Peterson would prefer working-class women and men fighting against each other, rather than holding the rich to account. They have successfully convinced many that capitalism is natural and that any attempt to think or act differently is undermining the order of things.

But as we have seen with this pandemic and the world wars that came before it, there is no natural progression. It is a myth. Our ideas come from our changing circumstances, the ebb and flow of history which is not like a straight line but more like an episode of Doctor Who jumping all over the place.

You often hear that capitalism is natural because we as humans are greedy and look out for our own economic interests, but maybe this behaviour is a reflection of the system that we live in. If you see a monkey dancing in a circus, is that the monkey's nature?

We have seen with the covid-19 pandemic that there are selfish people, but there are also good people who are willing to stay in their homes for months on end so that the health system doesn't collapse. We see millions volunteering and our neighbours and family helping each other out. There are many 'human natures' and choosing a few examples to justify a system that is systematically flawed as well as morally wrong, is how the rich and powerful use ideology to justify their actions.

On the 29th April 2020, the Financial Times predicted that the equivalent of 300 million full-time jobs could be lost worldwide because of the 2019 coronavirus pandemic.

The UN, which provided the figures, estimated that of the 64 countries that had implemented lockdown procedures so far, 1.6 billion people would be affected. That is more than the whole population of China and just over 19% of the world's population in 2020. Those affected would be mainly people working in the gig economy that has become more widespread over recent years as companies seek to cut workers' pay and increase their hours in the search of bigger profit margins. [1]

As economist Thomas Piketty explains in his book *Capital in the 21st Century*, relative returns from investments, including inherited wealth, are outpacing economic growth: the amount of value created by the economy. In other words, people who own things accumulate more from this, when compared with the income working people get from earning a salary. Thus, income from things such as inheritance, property, and money received from investments like shares, is less evenly distributed than income from working. These two factors combined have increased income inequality.

Furthermore, Piketty explains that this has always been the case since the 19th century, but it is the gap that matters. There has always been a slight gap throughout recent history, even more so since modern capitalism, however it did narrow. Following the first and second world wars when 90% tax rates were not seen as satanic, tax was used to distribute wealth more evenly. Now that the economy is slowing, and we are not taxing multinationals a lot, we are on a path to return to the economic situation of the 19th century. Those in power and wealth will keep it whilst the rest of us get poorer. The way of reversing this in the short term is taxes, in the long term a new societal system of redistribution. [2]

We should also add that income inequality increases dissatisfaction within nations, increases rates of health and social care problems, and it also stunts social mobility and economic growth. It disproportionately affects the working class, minorities, and women.

The USA has the fourth highest rate of income inequality, the gap between the lowest and highest earners, of the 38 OECD countries, these are all countries with market economies often referred to as 'developed countries'. Out of the developed countries, it also has the highest levels of health and social care problems, from the number of prisoners to mental health issues. It is not about how poor or rich a country is, but about the gap between the richest and the poorest. [3]

This makes us question the very concept of developed and developing countries and makes us question the mantra of growth and wealth, being the individual and collective markers of success.

What about healthy societies that are harmonious, work smarter and play more?

The UK is 9th of the OECD countries for income inequality. However, there is also another concept called wealth inequality which is who owns the wealth in a country (compared to how their income is generated as we have spoken of above).

In the UK, wealth is even more uneven when compared to income. In 2020 the richest 10% owned 43% of all wealth in the country versus the poorest 50% which only owns 9%. In 2023 the richest 50 families in the UK owned more wealth than half of the whole population, 33.5 million people. [4]

But if this is the case then why are the British public not making a fuss?

- This is the power of ideology and hegemony. Numerous polls over the years have shown that the British population is wrong about almost everything. This is not only a question of intelligence, but more a case of poor information. One recent poll in 2022 found that half of Brits think young people can't afford a home because they spend their money on things like Netflix and takeaways.

- Other big misconceptions from a popular poll back in 2013 suggested that the public believed that of every 100 pounds worth of benefits, 24 pounds were fraudulently claimed. In fact, it is 70p.

- They also believed that 31% of the population were immigrants when it was 13%.

- If you include migrants without legal paperwork, it was 15%.

- Regarding ethnicity, they thought black and Asian people made up 30% of the population, when in fact it was 11%.

- They were also wrong about the crime rates, believing that the crime rate had not fallen when it was actually 19% lower.

- The public believed the rate of teenage pregnancy was 25 times higher than it was. 0.6% of teenage girls became pregnant every year, not the 15% that was self-reported in the poll. [5]

But, clearly, when you have poor information, or skewed information, along with long-held biases, stereotypes, subjective points of view limited by what is around you, conspiracy theorists on the internet, falling living standards, a rapidly changing world and a ruling ideology that encourages rivalry, individualism and the monetisation of every aspect of life, it is easy to see why people are angry and often wrong.

Neoliberalism has convinced us that there is no alternative, thus taking away any agency we might have once had in political parties or unions. With this we are left to choose between various types of right-wing media all at various stages of reactionary views. Not only have they convinced us that this is the best it will get, but also that any change will likely threaten our 'way of life'. By pushing their ideology, they have made right wing reactionary opinions become acceptable even when they are contradictory and based on sensationalised themes instead of facts.

The coronavirus has put on display the injustices and inequalities in our society, in many cases it will also accelerate these problems and make them more widespread. It has exposed class divides that many had convinced themselves no longer existed.

One OECD report stated that *"The risk of COVID-19 infection for people living in the most deprived areas was at least 50% higher than among those living in the least deprived areas in six countries. In the United States and Australia, the risks of COVID-19 infection among people living in the most deprived areas were more than 3 times as high as those living in the least deprived areas. In Ireland, United Kingdom (Northern Ireland, Scotland and England), Spain (Barcelona) and Italy, the risk of COVID-19 infection in the most deprived areas was between 10% and 50% higher than in the least deprived areas"*. [6]

Never had it been easier to spot the working class from the rest. Most jobs that involved going outside during the pandemic involved manual labour. Some healthcare professionals aside, when most people in Europe were confined to their homes, because of the risk of hospitals collapsing, the people that did go to work were mostly low-paid people that work with their hands; dustbin men, cleaners, shop assistants, carers, takeaway workers, Amazon delivery drivers, hospital porters, nurses, and taxi drivers. The majority of people that could work from home, who were not all 'middle class', probably don't consider themselves 'working class' either. And even then, if you look a little closer, it shows you how most of us would struggle without the help of the state.

Most people who were unable to work because of the pandemic relied on their pay being subsided by the government. Not forgetting other measures legislated to help the system function. These movements alone prove that the government is capable of moving quickly to relieve society's problems. Much of it is down to political will. Here we see the economic mantras of neoliberalism such as limited state intervention, managing sectors of the market and letting them deliver, and, not forgetting, austerity all fall face down in the mud. Despite this the ideas based around neoliberalism regarding individualism, fake meritocracy and that there being no alternative to capitalism, all still persist in the minds of many as if nothing has happened. Here is where ideology steps in.

These myths of the markets have real consequences, such as the outsourcing of manufacturing to poorer countries has done the West no favours. Suddenly, when we needed protective gloves, aprons, and masks for health staff, every country (that had underfunded their health system due to the austerity imposed following the 2008 financial crisis) was clambering for materials from the East. Even then, Western governments turned to private companies to develop track and trace systems, ventilators, and vaccines. Governments literally threw money at them, and most companies never delivered. There are only a handful of success stories, and likely thousands of stories of corruption to come out.

21st century imperialism and its sibling, monopoly state capitalism, are both in crisis. With the coronavirus, many questioned what was happening; others embraced the change and hoped for more, and some are still doing all they can to return to normal. This is the battleground of ideology and for hegemonic rule in a time of crises.

What follows in this book is the simultaneous exploration of two of the woolliest, yet important concepts of our time: **neoliberalism** as the dominant mode of thought of our time or what is considered 'logical' and 'common sense' and **ideology**; and the way in which we can question, explore, attack, and hopefully overcome the former.

This book is structured to help the reader understand how ideology operates on the individual and on a societal level. We will also look at hegemony from a political viewpoint. There are many strands to hegemony but here we will only cover the basics that are liked with mainstream politics.

Later the book explores the lines of thought and history that makes up neoliberalism. You will hear me say that neoliberalim is dead. Economically it has been dying for a while and it has come in various forms switching between the reactionary and progressive forms and even taking on the form of populist politics. It is important to examine this form of politics and the development of ideology. This is because, like literary styles or music genres, ideology is not a clean-cut group of ideas, but something built up over time, gains momentum, reacts to the material world and adapts to new events. We have to look at it as something in progress: something dialectical. Therefore, if we want to know what comes after neoliberalism, we need to know where it is coming from and where it is heading.

Hegemony and Ideology

"My dear, religion is like a penis. It's a perfectly fine thing for one to have and take pride in, but when one takes it out and waves it in my face, we have a problem." -Maggie Smith

Antonio Gramsci was an Italian philosopher and politician imprisoned by Mussolini in 1926. In prison for the last 11 years of his life, he wrote 30 notebooks worth of theories and thoughts on Marxist philosophy, politics, and Italian nationalism. Whilst there he developed Marx's concept of ideology and his own concept of cultural hegemony, both of which remain important today.

Wait. Wait. *What is ideology?* It is how you form your view of the world and relate to it. It is literally how we see, judge, and interact with reality.

The word ideology has been repurposed over the years. Its original meaning is the study of ideas in the world. Later, and to this day, it has been used to describe approaches to society and beliefs on how it should be organised. (To be a fascist, a liberal, or to have a socialist idea). Furthermore, in the modern age, it has become a slur to use against people who think differently from us, and outside of the accepted common sense.

There are various major political ideologies: liberalism, socialism, conservatism, fascism, and communism. These *-isms* cross over and diverge on various topics such as how society is organised, how economic markets should function, what is ethical or legal, the role of the state, and who gets what and when. They each have their characteristics, often organised into the right, centre, and left political ideologies, which many of you are probably aware of.

Often, they battle over the meaning of concepts such as 'freedom' and 'responsibility' and have different views on how to organise society both on a practical level like *whether religion should be part of the school curriculum* and on ethical levels such as abortion. But to take the concept of ideology further, the study of ideology is the exploration of how these ideas collide in our reality. On the news, in the pub, in science journals, in the management of pandemics, and even within ourselves. Ideology is everywhere. This analysis is ideological.

That's why learning about it is so important. So when someone starts to mouth off in the pub about small boats, or scroungers you can eloquently tell them that they are full off shit and peddling the ruling class's ideas for them.

We can never leave ideology, but we can question it. To distinguish between the political ideologies, and where they sit in the world today, I have chosen various labels and theories from across the board to help structure this reflective account of ideology. It will also set the basis for further writings on a range of issues.

Gramsci says that ideology, of which today's dominant one is called neoliberalism, is how most of society relates to the world, from its values to deciding how society should function and be organised. Our subjective reality is partly constructed by ideology; often it is referred to as the glasses with which we see the world, but that cannot be removed; you can, however, change the lenses or even break them. [7].

We are influenced by ideology as we dialectically develop our identity by flowing in and out of society and back into ourselves. This is done by wanting to be a part of the world whilst at the same time wanting to build an individual identity for ourselves as human beings. When I was younger, I wanted a Game Boy to play Pokémon like everyone else, but obviously I didn't want the same colour console as my brother whose console was pink.

In my head pink was for girls, not boys. But this only started in the 1940s. Before both girls and boys wore white and later pink and blue, with the *Ladies Home Journal* later stating that *"the generally accepted rule is pink for the boys, and blue for the girls."* Yes: for a while pink was the colour for boy's. This shows how we must approach ideology. Not as a rule of set values and beliefs, the normal way we discuss someone's political ideology, but more as something that is fluid, time specific, often contradictory, and as something that holds certain features that mark it from other traditions. Furthermore, we should not confuse it with hegemony which we will come to later. Yet, we should mention here that ideas don't just organically emerge, they are forced up on us by people with power and influence [8]

Sometimes, if an ideology only covers a specific area, such as feminism or nationalism, they are called *thin* ideologies. They don't concern themselves with the big questions of who gets what and how, but they concentrate on more specific questions like how to make the world more equal for men and women. Often, they are attached to or interpreted by bigger ideologies which morph with them or reinterpret them in various ways. Whilst ideologies are not everything, such as love, it influences everything from whom we find attractive to how we structure our families. This also changes over time. Fat men were thought to be rich and powerful less than 100 years ago; now they are seen as unhealthy, lazy, and poor. The same could be said for the changing attitudes regarding women's roles in society and towards different races. But like the old, outdated stereotypes of women being delicate and caring, some of these ideas still persist in various societies and often in different forms of language.

Often, the dominant ideology directs how society is constructed economically, we call this the *economic base*. Economics here is talking about political economy, who has the power over the way that society produces things, who owns it, and who exploits who, often referred to as the means of production.

The dominant ideology is often a combination of various political ideologies working together to keep a system that benefits the ruling classes in place; at the moment, in most countries, this includes economic liberals and conservatives. This economic base is not just concerned with how we use money, but also who owns the businesses (communists and socialists believe the workers should own the companies, whereas liberals and conservatives believe that individuals can), where the profits go, and what the purpose of the various project are (to help people or for profit). Are profits going to shareholders, the state, or the workers? How is work directed and what are society's priorities? Why are the profits going to shareholders and not being reinvested into making the workplace more efficient and safer?

The economic base is managed by the ruling class, and supported by most of the other classes that enjoy its current form. They sustain their dominance via hegemony. This economic base influences the larger structures in society, often referred to as the *superstructure*. These include culture, nationality, stereotypes, parenting skills, teaching methods, sleep patterns, attitudes towards work, people's anxiety, the police, courts, laws, ethics, the media, parliament, society's health and social care problems, what we think beauty is, and our prejudices. This influence is not just one way: these structures reinforce the economic base and justify its very existence. It is a yin-yang type of relationship; both need each other to exist, and should one change, it can influence or change the other.

Gramsci's interpretation of this was that the superstructure, both civil and political parts of it, are a reflection of the economic base's form. An example is the slave trade. Laws, markets, businesses, magazines, boats, prices, practices, opinions for and against, supply chains, stereotypes, fiction and books were all part of the superstructure that made the slave trade legal and reinforced its reproduction. Moreover, the ideas that Africans and other non-white races are inferior to white Europeans also developed alongside the slave trade. These tropes still exist in our stereotypes today despite being thoroughly disproven. [9]

Over time, as the material economic base changes (who owns what and how things are produced and by whom), so does the superstructure and ideology that helps us interpret this reality. Ideology arises from material changes that come before it. As history moves forwards, the ruling classes of the time must form new alliances and fight ideological battles to maintain their dominance. These ideologies carry their own historical and regional differences. Often, their alliances and their legacy will affect how they deal with events that arise as part of the course of history.

Large ideologies do not fall overnight, but they are often built of various strands of ideologies that fight for dominance within the dominant ideology itself, a bit like footballers in the same team trying to become top goal scorer. Neoliberalism has been doing this at a fast pace more so since the contradictions in its own ideology have become apparent.

Following the neoliberal wave, social democratic parties started adopting its policies and much later become unpopular as a result of this move. However, more recently, neoliberalism has resorted to more reactionary stances on cultural matters such as immigration, class, and education. So much so that the economic practices continue in many institutions but in the markets, they are not so popular. In 2022, Liz Truss was effectively vetoed by multinational finance monopolies as they didn't like her Margaret Thatcher tribute act. She lasted just over six weeks as Prime Minister.

A quick note on the dominant ideology: We live in liberal democracies which were established following the capitalist revolutions such as the French Revolution.

On a wider more longer-term analysis, liberalism is the historical ideology of the West as its structures persist to this day as do many views which the majority of the populations have in common. Often these are seen as fundamental beliefs such as freedom of speech, the vote for everyone, rights to private property and so on.

The dominant ideology of the day has to interpret this history and make it part of its own world view, thus making its ideas seem natural and inevitable. This is why many centrist dads or 'objective' liberals pretend they are not 'infected' with ideology, when in fact they are deeper in it than anyone as they refuse to acknowledge their own ideas and where they come from.

Marxists have debated for years how to change society. Some say you can just change the economics and society will follow whilst others say you have to change society first.

However, Che Guevara's quote on this remains the most pertinent:

"Socialism cannot exist without a change in consciousness resulting in a new fraternal attitude toward humanity, both at an individual level, within the societies where socialism is being built or has been built, and on a world scale, with regard to all peoples suffering from imperialist oppression."

Thus, this is to say that the revolution inside the head has to come first, yet this does not mean we just say what we believe and hope for the best. We have to organise, intervene and educate to do this. Human agency is being able to change things, and with this comes a dialectic interaction between the individual and society. Realising the potential of an idea is the first step but carrying it through and changing ourselves has to be a part of the wider transformation of society.

A very bad football analogy

Forms of political ideologies are like football teams; they are always changing positions and want to stay at the top of the league. The positions in the league are different, and there can only be one champion.

Since the Premier league was started in 1992, Manchester United have won the title 13 times. They were the dominant team in the league for over 20 years until around 2013. I remember as a kid their fans were called glory hunters. Everyone wants to continue to be the dominant ideology. The one that tries to maintain its dominance over mainstream opinion and thought. To be and remain the common-sense choice. In those 20 years, mainly when Alex Ferguson was manager, if you said that United would one day in the future be a second-rate team in the Premier league, then fans would have looked at you oddly. It was only when Ferguson left that the team started to unravel, this started to become a possibility. New teams started to become likely champions. The big four became the big six and even Leicester City won the league. The same could be said for neoliberalism and the financial crisis of

2008. Dominance does not last forever; the ideologies become part of history. History is the story of class struggle. The master and slave narrative.

Common Sense

When I talk about common sense, I mean how people judge if a decision, approach, or if their opinion is within the boundaries of being acceptable and realistic for most of that society. What might be deemed an excellent investment in northern Europe may be considered too self-interested in China, or as not going far enough in the USA. What is considered a good idea or common sense can change depending on the dominant ideology and those ideas that challenge it. Slavery was once thought of as normal, and gay marriage was looked upon as immoral. The two have traded places. This is changing ideology, but as you can see, it doesn't happen on its own. The dominant ideas of the day change with history, and just like with the football teams, they need to be challenged and debunked. Here the human agency of the challengers and debunkers is key. We cannot just let history run its course and pray for socialism, that is why we have a rich history of people willing to stand up and shout 'We've had enough of this shit!'.

They are not all rebels and renegades, many are working men and women who took a stand, argued what they believed in and organised in their class. This is how change is made, not by 'great men', but by people.

This makes up the world of ideology, the battle over ideas and widening, or narrowing, the scale upon which people discuss and accept certain opinions. In political jargon, this is called the Overton Window. These discussions can range from a chat in a bar between friends about whether the country needs to have a king, or maybe they are presented in the form of a newspaper article which may give an opinion about whether leaving an international institution is a good idea or not. At certain times, topics will be more acceptable to people than others (like free broadband for everyone before and after the pandemic). What might have sounded like a crazy idea in the 80s or 90s, will now be considered normal or even 'backward' for not doing it. Teaching sex education that includes LGBTQ+, whilst it seems strange to some, will hopefully be normalised and de-politicised in years to come; in certain parts of the world that would be difficult to envisage. Hegemony is regional, cultural, and time orientated.

We live in a great time of hegemonic change. Look at how since around 2007 the Scottish National Party took over as the main force in Scottish politics. With Labour's turn towards neoliberalism and its neglect of most places outside of London, the SNP were able to replace them as the hegemonic force. This is not always reflected in electoral politics as they lost the independence referendum in 2015 but came back stronger than ever afterwards when Nicola Sturgeon became leader. Since her resignation this hegemonic status has been called into question. It's not just the policies and the votes that matter, it is the representation and the ability to co-opt old values, and traditions whilst also building power. This is done by active and passive consent. People accepted the SNP's hegemonic rule because they believed in the legitimacy of democracy and parliament.

Creating and exploiting those moments is when ideology really comes to the forefront and can change public opinion. Colliding forces will try to push their ideology, or try to negotiate for concessions to their views, thus changing the landscape on which they compete. One of the best examples of this in British politics was Jeremy Corbyn's ability to bring up imperialism following the Manchester bombing attack. Following a suicide bomb attack at a music concert during the 2017 General Election, Corbyn was able to highlight the role in which the West had played in destabilising the Middle East. A view not shared by many in his party, yet it was one that resonated with people. By doing this, for a short time, he was able to change the conversation that normally follows such events. He took a hammering for this move from his own party, and the usual suspects continued with their Islamophobic rhetoric, but he was able to give another point of view that questioned Britain's role in destabilising the Middle East.

There are also battles within ideologies (both the dominant ideology and the opposing ones) for different internal strands of that ideology to become the leading force. Brexit, for example, was about fighting for the direction of the Conservative party. Remember, David Cameron held the EU referendum to appease Eurosceptics and to gain a few UKIP voters. What they didn't bank on was the level of alienation in the population towards political institutions and bourgeoisie politics which the EU is the perfect example of.

When a similar vote was held to join the European Community/ Common Market back in 1975 the left of the Labour Party, Tony Benn and Michael Foot and the Communist Party of Great Britain included, were against Britain's membership of what would become the EU. During the 2017 referendum to leave, the left that supported Brexit were sidelined by the hard right.

The Conservatives are always fighting in their party; some members are more globalist whilst others are more nationalist. In the British Labour Party, the battle is often between right-wing neoliberals, soft-left reformists and socialists. The right sabotaged Jeremy Corbyn's leadership for over 4 years and still continues to demonise him to this day. I am sure if you are reading this book, you know this tale, if you don't take a look at the film *Oh, Jeremy Corbyn- The Big Lie.*

Macro-ideological battles happen within ideologies, but when it comes down to the bigger match against an opposing ideology, it is normally about who can get more people to agree with them and work together.

The right are often better at this than the left as they are defending a system that benefits them and is already in place whilst the left are trying to replace it, hence all the splits in left-wing parties: they all think their theory is the best way to replace capitalism. [10] [11]

Why does it matter if certain opinions are acceptable or not? Because they persuade people to vote a certain way, they can push people to join groups or protests, support initiatives, sign petitions, and can even dictate the validity of a revolution. The dominant ideology also has to keep its finger on the pulse. Before the 2022 elections, French President Emmanuel Macron was ramping up his Islamophobic rhetoric, hoping it would play in his face-off against famous far-right bigot Marie Le Penn.

The people who don't agree with the dominant ideology often form an opposing worldview. This is called a radical or opposition ideology. They often have to build a coalition of opposing groups to build a viable alternative to whoever the ruling class is. If they play the game correctly, then they can become the dominant ideology. However, this depends on the thing they are trying to change. Often at elections or during large events, they will try to convince various groups, and other smaller ideologies, to agree with them and to change public discourse in their favour, and, if possible, overturn the dominant ideology. Often these coalitions of ideas form the basis for the future society, but even after winning an election, or cutting off the head of the king, the ideology has to fight on to cement itself. Furthermore, we only call it a revolution when the dominant group changes the make-up of society, and more specifically the economic base. The threat of revolution is what causes things such as fascism to rise, which was historically funded by companies and supported by the middle classes, but also conspiracy theories that have no basis in reality. Fascism, and other counter-revolutionary forces such as Margaret Thatcher and Ronald

Regan, use revolutionary language to sell the promise of security and prosperity to the working classes, when in actual fact they are taking away any previously hard fought for gains.

Hegemony is the name of the battleground (or the football league if you will). Sections of society battle for hegemonic dominance to influence ideological change. This might be on specific topics to sway public opinion in their favour to get a law changed. Yet, it is not always about the bigger battle to become the dominant team, in fact, more often than not, it is the smaller battles that matter, building up and changing public opinion bit by bit. It can push society in various ways, with distinct parts battling over the hegemonic areas. Or in other cases, such as the Russian Revolution, some groups can seize the opportunity to take power quickly. In the case of Russia, this happened only when the ruling class and their dominant ideology had been completely discredited. The idea that there was no alternative to the Tsar of the time had been put to bed with their management of the war and their defeat. The slogan '*Land, Peace and Bread*' resonated with the starving soldiers who helped with the revolution.

Lenin says that revolution can only take place in certain circumstances: the ruling class can no longer rule anymore, the working class is not prepared to accept their rule and, thirdly, that the working class is organised to take control.

Revolution can be on the streets or at the ballot box. This is another reason why the ruling class must maintain its dominance, for fear of revolution, even if this means giving concessions. You didn't think they just gave us the welfare state and weekends for free, did you?

To sum it up in a phrase: hegemony is best thought of as the battle for the leadership of society.

Ideological State Apparatuses

Louis Althusser, a French structural Marxist, came up with the theory of ideological state apparatus building further on Gramsci's work. He claims that these apparatuses are used to maintain ideological dominance. They are part of, and keep the form of, the superstructure. He splits the apparatus into two forms: ideological apparatus, such as family, religion, education, culture, the media, politics, law, and various others. They work by reproducing and reinforcing the dominant ideology's beliefs and ideas which we individually come to terms with. Each arm has a separate function, such as entertainment, which keeps us hooked to Netflix rather than forming a union and demanding higher wages. There are parts that have no link to the economic base of course.

He says that, without a doubt, education is the most important arm. It teaches children to be 'good citizens' and obey the rule of law. It makes us obedient and also gives us the skills we need to work in the capitalist system. This is how capitalism reproduces itself and its ideology. Let's face it: where else can you get someone's attention for 8 hours a day for 12 years or more?

Before schools, it was the church that acted as the main ideological apparatus; you can still see its legacy in society today and in some parts of the world it remains a key source of ideology. An interesting example is the way the Spanish Civil War is taught in schools. In the summer of 1936, following a coup by the army, Hitler's Nazis, and Mussolini's blue shirts, Spain entered a bloody civil war. The democratically elected republic was overthrown. Francisco Franco became the country's dictator until his death in 1975. Throughout his era and even until today, the teaching of the civil war has been controversial and heavily contested by the Spanish right. From school textbooks, and street names to the lack of a national museum, the education around this issue remains poor and very partisan. If the truth were really taught well then, the country's whole history of the past, and that of which it is yet to write, would all be dramatically altered. The same should be said for the British Empire and the history of the trade union movement. It isn't just if it is taught but how, where, and when.

Then there is repressive state apparatus, such as the police and the army that enforces the dominant ideology via threat, and at times, actual violence. However, this does not have to be in the form of a police truncheon; just knowing that it is there has enough power to encourage citizens to follow the rules. It could be that you mess around at school, don't follow the rules, and get poor grades. This then excludes you from university or well-paying jobs - thus the threat of a poor lifestyle encourages participation, and therefore support, of the dominant ideology. Anti-union laws are a further example of repressive state apparatus as they put barriers in the way of forming collective action. [12]

We should note here that the superstructure is not wholly responsive to the economic base, it can alter it. Hence why any threat of democratic change or hostility that may threaten the existing state of things is set up on by the right-wing media and the government. Language and symbolism are a huge part of the battle, with ideologies weaponising and using language and symbols to maintain, or influence, the opposing one. Each ideology has unique views on topics and ultimately the word and vocabulary associated to it. Equality in neo-liberal speak means everyone gets what they have based upon merit (despite some people getting ahead start by being rich), whilst in socialism it means helping to level the playing field. Freedom for libertarians means freedom from government interference in all forms, whereas for a communist it means being free from capitalism's wage slavery and the threat of homelessness. For example, in Spain, during the pandemic, there has been a battle over the symbols of nationalism with certain political parties trying to wield the national flag and constitution to get people to agree with their vision of the country.

Furthermore, the Communist Party of Britain sets out a very different view of patriotism when compared to the Conservatives or Labour. It is one of teaching the horrors of colonialism and imperialism and one that celebrates the wins and sacrifices of the British working classes of the past. However, this is where the dominant ideology of the right has it easier as they celebrate the Empire and don't make people feel guilty for their country's past. [12]

Often the dominant ideology will assimilate what it cannot conquer. From mobile phones for children to Pride, over time it all becomes part of society's normal life or common sense. It appears as part of the natural progress of time. Not that everyone accepts it, but consensus outweighs the minority view. That said, there are also regional forms of ideology. The perfect example of this is when the majority of Western companies change their logo to rainbow colours for Pride in June, yet if you look at their accounts in the Middle East, the logo won't be changed.

Ideology changes, sometimes only slightly, depending on various factors. This may influence how we act or how we perceive things and customs. Anyone who has lived abroad will probably tell you it has changed them; they had a taste of a different ideology. These interactions with ideas can fuse with various other ideologies or past ideological beliefs left over from earlier dominant ideas (such as what it means to be a man or American), experiences and values are built into our identities.

The whole population takes part in the hegemonic battle, whether they know it or not. In the past this was done via several routes from the church: "We are all sinners and must repent!" to the ranks of the army: "Our nation is superior to others".

Nowadays this is done via the media, education, and state institutions. The aim of this battle is to turn the dominant ideology into culture, making it appear natural to everyone. Making it common sense.

There are individuals that play a part in this process. Gramsci called them organic intellectuals. They are not intellectuals like the stuffy Oxford type, but individuals from both the ruling and lower classes, that take part in public life, via the media or via social institutions, countering public discourse and therefore influencing public opinion. In the modern day this could go from Piers Morgan to a person holding court on Twitter.

So how am I influenced by apparatus and ideology?

Althusser claimed that apparatuses interpolate the citizens with ideology. Interpellation is the concept that humans are presented with an idea, and they come to believe in it, almost like they come to think of it as their independent thought and opinion. This is easy when parents, teachers and news presenters don't offer an alternative or a weak one at best. This is also why none of us are the same, but we hold similar beliefs. We have different influences. The apparatus presents the ideology and sways us to believe in it. We, as the subject, believe (or sometimes not) in the ideology. It becomes the way we see things - as we said before, the common sense. It does this by subconsciously influencing you and society itself. You end up believing the ideology; it doesn't brainwash you. You choose to believe it, even though sometimes you can see the cracks in the system that the ideology is masking. That is why we are cynical towards the system and make jokes about it, but nevertheless carry on going to work and paying bills. It is the individuals' and societies' belief in the system and their behaviour which reproduces the society that keeps it alive. Equally, it is their disbelief that can end it. Yet, as Marxist philosopher Slavoj Zizek points out, believing in the ideology is not enough, and often we don't fully, but it is the actions we carry out, that are influenced by what we think, that really keep the system going. [13]

When the ideology becomes the new common sense, it becomes part of how we see the world, it primarily does this via language, as this is how we communicate ideas. Capitalism has done this so well that it appears natural; in fact, if you present people with an ideological idea, like abolishing private education, they may question it, but if it appears natural, like when austerity was presented like a household budget and a natural choice, then it is a lot easier to accept subconsciously. There is a lot more on how people assimilate ideology, and it is still heavily debated by academics, but it is not the aim of this book.

These ideas are obviously not fixed, and the battle for ideological dominance is always swaying. An example would be teaching about homosexuality in schools. As religion loses any dominance it once had, and progressive groups push for more representation in society, one group will take over another, but as you have probably seen it is not straight forward. Ecology is an example of an ideology that has become more prominent because of international material problems coming into the public domain. This shows that ideologies can be dormant for a time and rise when their ideas become the answers to the problems the society faces. It's the dominant ideology's job to find its own answer or sweep aside the problem. It must do this before another popular ideology challenges its position. This is a hegemonic battle to retain power.

An example is socialism absorbing ecology to be a part of its hegemonic bloc to challenge the ruling neo-liberal ideology. Neoliberalism can either adopt its own position to counter it or it can downplay and oppose it. Donald Trump denying climate change is an obvious example.

Gramsci claims that a revolution cannot be successful unless oppressed groups agree on an alternative ideology to the current dominant one. This has not been done since the neoliberal counter revolution. We fight to build class consciousness and overthrow the blood sucking vampiristic capitalists.

To summarise, ideology and hegemony are not linear concepts, just like history and time. In the words of the Doctor when talking about time: *"People assume that time is a strict progression of cause to effect, but *actually* from a non-linear, non-subjective viewpoint - it's more like a big ball of wibbly wobbly... time-y wimey... stuff."* The same can be said for ideology and the hegemonic football league.

How are ideologies constructed?

To steal a phrase from Shrek, it is better to think of ideology like an onion, they have layers (but in two ways). The first being time related. Ideologies build on and assimilate the ideology that comes before it, and before that and before that. This builds traditions and the illusion that things have always been this way (unless there has been a revolution of some form). They have to appear natural to be accepted or seen as a popular change. A common-sense idea fitting into the framework of an ever-moving window of acceptability.

The other layers are for the analysis of ideology. The three levels include doctrine, belief, and ritual. The **doctrine** concerns the theories and ideas that underpin the ideology. In neoliberalism this would be the work of Friedrich Hayek and Milton Friedman, and the beliefs of 19th century liberals that had been handed down to their modern-day counterparts. The narrative that comes from the doctrine often claims to be the best way to naturally organise the world, because it complements 'human nature'.

The **belief** layer concerns the structure that is there to reinforce beliefs in the ideology, such as the ideological and state apparatus as described by Althusser. This might include a constitution, parliament, and stock markets. These reinforce the ideological doctrine's narrative that is taken on by the subject. A constitution may turn into a sublime object, something that is considered beyond debate, beyond ideology, when in fact it keeps everything in place.

The third layer of **ritual** becomes complicated and reflects into itself. Thus, it stops being a big ball of ideas and become an idea in itself. Marx's theory of commodity fetishism is the perfect example. Marx said that money, like many other commodities, has qualities that are not material. Instead of being a direct reflection of the commodity, like the paper it is printed on (or in the case of yachts, with the rich having enormous impractical ones) we are attracted to the worth of the object in a phantasmic form. Money's embodiment is wealth (the yacht depends on its size; the bigger the better), but money is just paper (and the yachts, no matter what size it is; it is still a boat). We know this, but at the end of the day we still act like it isn't, even though we know it is. This is because ideology turns money into a commodity, it can never be just paper to us. This is how ideology guides us and our views about certain things. And even if we reject this way of living, then we are merely just stepping into another ideology. [13]

My favourite example of this from my childhood was Pokémon cards. Was that shiny piece of card with Charizard written on it really worth 16 pounds (the guy had a pile of them behind the desk). Yet, if the children's parents turned around and told them they were stupid for wanting that expensive card, you can bet that one of them would not flinch at buying branded clothes or food.

As I previously said, ideology is not everything. Terry Eagleton puts this clearly by saying, *"Not everything in a culture is ideological, though anything in it might become so."*[14]

Why all this fuss over ideology?

Following the fall of the USSR in 1991, George Bush Senior announced that the battle between ideologies was over. Capitalism had won. This led to the theory called *the End of History* by political philosopher Francis Fukuyama. Here he claimed that liberal democracy was the ideal form of governance for all nation states and that we had arrived at this position because of the fall of other alternatives. Obviously, the Marxists never agreed.

It has been clear since the financial crisis of 2008, and even more so during this pandemic, that we live in an ideological world whether centrist dads like it or not. The ideological battles may have been quieter in the 90s, but they are not planning to get any quieter from here on out.

Creating the Illusion: The Birth of Neoliberalism

"Underlying most arguments against the free market is a lack of belief in freedom itself."

Milton Friedman, Capitalism & Freedom (1962).

G20 Meltdown protest in London on 1 April 2009 (Jonny White, CC)

Via the manipulation of meritocratic values mixed with a misconstrued version of Darwin's theory of evolution used for political ends (commonly referred to as *Social Darwinism*), a change in our concept of freedom, changed our perception of the state's role in society, and pushing the narrative that humans are *homo economicus* (this is the idea that humans always act rationally and in their own economic self-interests), Neoliberalism, the name given to the ideology at this stage of state monopoly capitalism, tries to justify itself as natural (and very successfully) when in fact these things have become a contradiction into themselves.

State monopoly capitalism is the name given to the economic base of society. It is essentially a fusion of monopoly capitalism and the nation-state, or in terms of Europe the European Union.

There have been changes in its make-up over the years, however, the basis of this reality has been around since the 1920s: monopoly capital influences and at times dictates large areas of policy to democratically elected governments. Examples are rife with corporate lobbying gifts, meals and holidays to MPs only being the surface of the cesspool. The often-cited revolving door is the most obvious with MPs getting positions on boards after they stop working as MPs, and in many cases, they continue to have second jobs whilst claiming to represent their constituents.

Prime Minister David Cameron went to work for Greenshill Capital as an advisor after he quit. The same banker of the same name Australian Lex Greenshill was used as an advisor by Cameron when he was PM. Cameron was contracted to work for 25 days a year at an average rate of $40,000 per day. His job was to help the group secure government contacts.[15]

Corporations influence legislation that may harm profit margins and like during the Covid-19 epidemic, they are given golden contracts in areas they have never worked in before such as medical supplies or tracking apps. When this happens, and the electoral parties don't challenge the monopoly giants, it is easy to see why people feel powerless, angry and have no sense of solidarity, or collective power, and don't see the prospect of a different world.

This book is not about state monopoly capitalism, but it is an important point. Neoliberalism is the current ideology that maintains this dictatorship of capital.

Whilst these ideas have been disputed and heavily disproven on an academic and practical level, that does not change the fact that they remain central ideas to the ideology and have left marks on how people relate and view things. Unconscious bias towards certain groups, such as racial profiling by law enforcement or accepting the justification of austerity measures - that poorer people deserve to be poor and that they are in some way faulty, that a banker deserves to be paid more than a nurse- these are modern examples of how these ideas have become and remain prominent within our society.

This *common sense* has changed how people feel about low-paid workers, our views on how the government should support its citizens and how much it should be involved in the markets, furthermore it has become an excuse to give tax cuts to the rich. The demonisation of the working class in the form of reality television and the talk of benefit scroungers was a further push for a hyper-meritocratic view of society. This has allowed politicians of all stripes to cut back on the state and what it did for its citizens whilst making people feel bad for not 'making it'. This pandemic should have shown us that society cannot function without the working class, but also that it continues without stockbrokers and bureaucrats.

Growing Pains

Neoliberalism has a long history, but it was in the time of Margaret Thatcher and Ronald Reagan, the early 1980s, that it established itself in the UK and the USA. Since then, it has been pursued by successive governments in most countries, including some 'left' wing parties, and international institutions the world over. Think: the EU, World Bank, IMF and so on.

After the Second World War, when the USA, France and the UK were scrambling against the USSR to establish who would be the top dog in the world, 44 nations got together at the Bretton Woods summit to stabilise capitalism in the face of communism. Following the summit, there was a tremendous wave of investment into countries via the Marshall Plan, a series of large loans from the US to some European countries, and investment in the US itself. Many saw this as the US Empire laying economic foundations ready to take over as the new imperialist power after the British Empire had been dismantled. Capitalism was re-founded in many countries; they did this by implementing a progressive tax system on the rich, investing in trade and commodities, and expanding the welfare state, which many claim was due to the threat of revolt. Most countries started universal health care systems, and schools and made huge improvements in social housing, transport, and other amenities.

This was all after and during a time when capitalism did not look so natural. You had communism competing alongside and you also had the memory of the Great Depression from 1929-39. The USSR had defeated Nazi Germany and living standards were improving at a rapid pace. This is even more evident later towards the late 50s and 60s. We must remember that whilst it was the USA that made it first to the moon, at the time the USSR were ahead at other points putting the first satellite, the first animals and the first men and women into space.

After the Marshall plan had been set into action the era of liberal social democracy, or New Deal thinking, started and it was the dominant ideology until around the late 70s or mid-80s (many hail the 1968 Paris riots as a point where its hegemonic dominance started to kilter). This period after the war was essentially a pact between, capitalists, liberal politicians, and most of the centre-left. The right also supported some incentives. The basis of this ideology was that the market provided and met some of a country's needs, but also that the nation-state would be able to intervene. It was normal for the state to own key infrastructure (such as the health systems, trains, buses, mines, airlines, car brands, electricity companies, and the postal service) and run services for the sake of the country, not for profit. At its peak, the British government run all of these and even nationalised travel agents Lunn Poly. These ideas gave us the skeletons of the infrastructure we still see today. [12] The counterculture (yes, the hippies and that lot) were generally against 'the man' as they saw the state (both liberal democracy and communist countries) as oppressive. Freedom and peace were on the menu, but no one was serving it. Further subcultures would embrace rebellion. While we might think of communists today as rebels, they were in fact seen as hard workers and at times a bit 'square' as they might have said back then.

However, this New Deal ideology was not all-encompassing across the world, the USSR stood in opposition to liberal ideas with its version of communism. The Cold War was essentially a fight for hegemonic dominance but with nukes. Things changed after the USSR fell in the early 1990s: capitalism seemed to be the economic system of choice.

Not liking high taxes, the state running key industries, regulated markets, and holding the belief that man is at his best when his money and society were not regulated by the state, Friedrich Hayek formed the *Mont Pelerin Society*. A later key figure of neo-liberal thought, Milton Friedman would also join the group. Thus, the ideology of neoliberalism was (re)born. That is not to say they created the ideas around neoliberalism: they already existed; they just updated them and promoted them. Ideas come from material realities. The political and economic consensus around the New Deal ideology was coming apart due to an oil crisis and inherent contradictions within the system. With the socialist project stumbling in the USSR, the Vietnam War and various levels of discontent, a taste for the future became apparent. [16]

The wealthy and their politicians were looking for an alternative way to keep hold of their wealth and power and the system that gave them all that in the first place. At first, neoliberalism sounded absurd; it was only later that it got its shot. It was the answer they had been looking for. In the early 1970s Chile, Salvador Allende became one of the first self-proclaimed Marxists to be democratically elected as a President in Latin America. The CIA had already been involved as they were concerned about how a "well-functioning socialist experiment" could affect American markets and hegemony. Furthermore, Allende preached non-violence and wanted to use technology to help improve the functioning of the proposed planned economy. When it became apparent that they could no longer stop Allende by interfering with the country's democracy, they supported General Pinochet and the army to overthrow the government in a coup. A dictatorship was established and 4,000 people were murdered and 40,000 were tortured well after the coup had ended. A large number of these people were leftists. The coup was on the 11th of September and is often referred to as 'the other 9/11'.

Presidente Allende

The US didn't stop at overthrowing another country's government, it allowed neoliberal economists to experiment in the country. Often referred to as the 'Chicago Boys' due to their origins laying in Chicago University, these economists unleashed a series of economic reforms throwing the country into worse economic turmoil. They sold off publicly owned companies and oversaw strict austerity measures. They cut enormous parts of government expenditure and made many free trade agreements with other countries, whilst removing any trade barriers. With control over the political situation because of the military junta, the economists like Milton Friedman, run the country's economy like it were a computer simulation game. These changes led to mass inequality of which the effects are still felt today. Seeing that these policies made the rich richer, the IMF, World Bank and later Margaret Thatcher and Ronald Regan would follow their example.

The liberal part of the word comes from 19th century *Classical Liberalism:* the belief man is better when he can do as he pleases without government interference with an emphasis on the economic part. Hayek set up the society to see how they could go about reviving it. It should not be confused with *Social Liberalism,* the belief that people should be able to choose how they want to live, and that individual freedom should be respected by the government as much as possible, but, also that the state has a responsibility to address issues such as poverty and climate change. Social liberals feel they can do this without changing capitalism, but just by managing it better or making it more human-friendly.

Just to note, I use the word neoliberalism instead of late-capitalism, or even liberalism, as it is more specific regarding the problems of capitalism we face today and this specific way of thinking that has been reborn since the crumbing of the post-war consensus. The ideology has flourished more since the fall of the Berlin Wall and the USSR. This is also one of the problems with the dominant ideology of today. It is the new (neo) liberalist thought of the 21st century. There has always been an ideology, both before and after capitalism.

"The ideas of the ruling class are, in any age, the ruling ideas"

Karl Marx and Friedrich Engels (*The German Ideology*)

Doctrine for the Masses

Neo-liberals believe that the free market is the best way to organise society. They claim that the government should be just an administrator, not a supervisor or a player in the market, even to the point that private companies should provide services such as hospitals, schools, and prisons. They say they want a 'small state' that will not interfere in people's lives. This is a common misconception, or a sleight of hand, as under neo-liberal control the state is often used for the benefit of capital, rather than against it. It does this by creating new markets, initially by selling of the state's companies/shares, or by invading or coercing other countries to exploit their natural resources and economies. All whilst reducing what it did for citizens, often monetising services or cutting them. Basically it is using the state, its powers and resources to help people with money get more money, instead of helping the less fortunate or improving the lives of the citizens. (For more on this, read or watch the Shock Doctrine).

To justify their support for markets with minimal restrictions, they claim that the main interactions between people are 'economic' (*homo economicus*), or better put: that people always act in their own interests to increase their capital (whether that be economic, social, or cultural capital). It believes that this is the principal force behind human progress, and the individual drive for capital gain furthers progress in society. If this were true, then things such as Wikipedia would not exist. The internet may not have been given away by Tim Berners-Lee, and you might consider not having children. Of course, this is opposed to the view that it is groups of people, or collectives, that fuel the engine of history. By stating this view, they argue that any barriers stopping individual progress are stopping humanity from reaching its potential. They also love to talk about the great man version of history where one person moves the whole world forward alone, instead of talking about how classes and nations change the world. This is where the great myth of trickle-down economics starts.

Neoliberalism encourages competition between people. It states that individuals will always act in their own interests: therefore, if we allow competition, individuals will push further, thus increasing capital, improving standards, and making progress. You might think this is common sense, and it works in certain circumstances, but does it work in places such as hospitals? Schools? Competition like most things is okay within moderation. Whilst it may work with encouraging people to work harder, teams to work faster, or in certain places to improve standards, it does not work everywhere. Should it work to the extent that children get anxious over exam marks? Where students are refused by schools because of their low grades? Or to the extent you take work home with you because you want your team to perform well or risk losing your job?

An example I have seen whilst working as a nurse. By allowing separate companies to bid for the contract to run the service, the NHS had to compete with outside companies. Each company put forward a proposal. *We can treat X number of patients for Y amount of money.* Now the NHS never had to make money, only balance the books, whilst outside companies had shareholders who expected profits. The companies with better bids, often seen as more efficient, got the contracts. So now the service had the money from the health service, but they also had shareholders. Standards lowered as the service was treated more like a company than a clinic. Nurses left because of the tick-box nature of seeing patients, the demand to see more patients quicker and the watering down of their conditions. Visits and treatments were limited to some of the most vulnerable and at-risk patients in the community. It became a production line instead of a health service. The effects spread throughout the other services, with the voluntary sector, the police, the hospital, and mental health services filling in. Hardly efficient. We see the worst examples of this in the capitalist heartlands of the USA, where people go out of their way to work hard and not take holidays because of the fear of being replaced.

The same could be said for the privatisation of the UK's trains: standards lowered, and prices increased. Between 1994 and 1997 British railways were privatised: since then, the average price has gone up by at least 20% in real terms, and they have risen twice as fast as wages since 2009. Some fares have gone up by 300% since privatisation and it is estimated that the average UK citizen pays 5 times more in proportion to their salary when compared to the average European. Britain may have left the EU, but its train lines are all owned by European countries that make a profit out of it. A similar model is about to be rolled out all over the EU.[20]

This also tells us about the neoliberal way of justifying the selling off of public wealth. They underfund services to within an inch of their lives and then claim that privatisation is to make it more efficient. This happened with British Rail. It is often claimed as part of the wider British history that British Rail was inefficient, slow, never on time and plagued with state employee laziness. When in actual fact it was a fairly good system run on a shoestring. With what resources it had, it did well. Is the NHS going through something similar?

Furthermore, neoliberalism encourages the privatisation of public services as it believes that the market is more effective at managing them, which, given the amount of bureaucracy in working out who will provide what, this is easily contestable. I remember trying to get a light bulb replaced on a ward once. It took several phone calls, form filling, and in the end, it took 3 days to change the light bulb. Just think how many people that took. The person answering the phone, the electrician, the nurse to call and sign the paperwork, the person taking the paperwork to bill the NHS for changing the lightbulb and someone in the NHS to oversee the payment. And they say the USSR was bureaucratic, in fact, it was an argument for the modern-day self-managing market in the 80s, yet in the 2020s it has become a bureaucratic spider web.

The Public Finance Initiative (PFI) wasn't just hospitals either, most towns have a PFI legacy building in them whether that is a school, library, town hall, sports centre, or theatre. It is reported that one hospital was charged 5,500 pounds for a sink, a school was charged 25,000 pounds for 3 parasols, and a police force was charged nearly 900 pounds for a chair. Some PFI contracts won't finish until 2040. Most of this was brought in by Tony Blair's version of the Labour Party. [20]

Privatisation is the state working for capital, creating new markets, and not for the citizens that elect it. These actions have increased private wealth but decreased public resources and has curbed governments' abilities to deal with inequalities. It has led to companies getting so much money that they are no longer bothered by the state. They own so much that they can threaten to leave a country should a government want to do something that it does not agree with, like raising taxes or putting limits on pollution. Most of the time they push governments to water down policies that may affect their shareholders, such as fracking or health initiatives, and after all that the politicians get donations, gifts, free hospitality, money for campaigns, free trips, high fees for speeches and in some cases a job with them once they have left office. This is the essence of state monopoly capitalism.

Back to competition: it harbours teamwork and can spark creative thoughts. Yet, it can enlarge or deflate people's egos; it increases aggression and pits people against one another, despite them possibly being from unequal backgrounds. A student who has gone to the best schools and universities will have something over a person who got a job when leaving school or the student that never studied at school for various reasons outside of their control.

Yet whilst the values of competition are embodied in so called 'social mobility' (the act of improving your societal position) it is in fact in decline. Various factors contribute to this but the system is not working. The gap between children that are legible for free school meals and those who are not is demonstrated in their writing, reading and maths skills. Children who were eligible for free school meals because of their poorer background were less likely to reach level 2 for these skills in Key stage one (ages 5-6) in school. [21]

Furthermore, the London School of Economics has shown that absolute mobility (earning more than your father) has fell by 20 points since the 2008 financial crash. [22]

The idea of social mobility (versus the reality) reinforces the view of meritocracy and that 'you get what you deserve'. Not only that, but does everything have to be a competition? No, but increasingly we are seeing life more as a competition. You only have to look at social media to see this.

Meritocracy is the friendly face of competition. This is the belief that humans advance through life depending upon their individual achievements. What you put in; you get out. Whilst this sounds like common sense, and mostly it is, this idea has been hijacked. In doing this, neo-liberals have been able to keep alive old ideological values that had to be played down in the aftermath of the Holocaust. By installing values of hyper-meritocracy, they feed the myth of *Social Darwinism*. The view that some people are more evolved, superior, and thus have more value than others. There is a difference, but one that has been played on.

Social Darwinism is the 19th century theory that says certain sections of society are more evolved than others: essentially a misapplication of Darwin's theory of evolution. Herbert Spencer was the purveyor of this theory. He claimed that humans passed on poor qualities, such as how moral a person was, to their offspring. He argued that by regulating capitalism, we were slowing down the extinction of certain parts of the human race, the inferior parts. If we supported the poor, then they would continue to exist, as would their negative qualities that were undesirable. [23]

This train of thought was hugely influential in the Western world with liberals, social democrats, conservatives and fascists and was used to justify racism, slavery, capitalism, and the British Empire.

Eugenics, the pseudo-scientific term for this idea, was later embraced by the Nazis and was used as their justification for the holocaust killing between 17 to 19 million people. This included Jews, Soviet citizens and POWs, Eastern Europeans, disabled people, Freemasons, homosexuals, Romani and socialists and communists. Following the war, this form of science was all but abandoned by the scientific community. However, just because the exhibitions were removed, and it stopped being taught in universities, it does not mean that its influence has completely gone.

Eugenics has been highly disproven but still remains active in society. Its closely related narrative used to describe parts of society lingers in the media in tabloids, talk shows and people's opinions. Katie Hopkins's comment in The Sun, the UK's biggest newspaper, comparing refugees to cockroaches, is just one example. Elements of this viewpoint, often phrased as cultural differences, work their way into all media and influence public perception.

These ideological double standards come up when we look at how the government deals with societal issues, often depending on which group of people are involved. An example was pointed out by rapper and writer Akala on Good Morning Britain regarding the media's reporting and the government's management of knife crime in the UK. Both portraying it as an enormous problem in black London communities, whilst not highlighting the knife crime rates involving white people in the rest of the country.

Whilst rates in London were high, the media's commentary focused more on the colour of their skin as if the community were barbaric. Often this is framed as part of their 'culture' rather than their race. Culture is more difficult to identify and has less of a Nazi ring to it.

When Glasgow had the highest murder rate in Europe in the early 2000s, the fact that the people were white, or their culture, never became part of the conversation, it was treated as a wider problem in the society. Eventually, it was treated as a public health issue. The

Scottish government increased social support in the areas, and healthcare professionals worked with police; this has lowered the stabbing rates since.

Whilst that approach worked in Glasgow, the Conservative Party's approach in England was evidence of how they see problems from their own ideological perspective. They planned to put warnings on the side of fried chicken boxes to spread awareness. This was immediately highlighted as racial stereotyping that black men love fried chicken, and just goes to show how ingrained these beliefs are within the government. David Lammy, a black Labour MP, responded *"Is this some kind of joke?! Why have you chosen chicken shops? What's next, #KnifeFree watermelons?"*

These viewpoints could also be extended to the image of working-class people being uneducated, dirty, and culture-less, thus deserving to remain poor. The image of the *Jeremy Kyle Show, Benefit Street,* and *Shameless.* These are recycled images of reality, hyperreality. Sociologist Jean Baudrillard argues that the recycling of these images in the media led to a hyperreality where the audience failed to separate fiction from reality, thus giving the impression that all council estates were like Benefits Street or all people on benefits are scamming the system. [24]

Here hyper-meritocracy has become the new social Darwinism. It fails to account for privileges and keeps the rich on top with a few token poor people being allowed to climb their way up to give the rest of us hope. Molly Mae, owner of Pretty Little Thing, millionaire, and influencer with six million followers likes to say things like *"we all have the same 24 hours in a day"*. This highly individualist approach to life is peddled to her millions of followers who want to be just like the Instagram star. There was a backlash against her comments but still, this Thatcherite narrative is toxic for the average person. We are told that if we 'get on the grind and hustle every day' we too can be as great, powerful, and rich as them. We can see here how the concept of freedom has been repurposed for the 21st century. Ignoring the idea that freedom is to be free of pain, poverty, persecution, free from worries about having a home or a job, or being free to say what you want, to protest and form unions. These freedoms, many of which feel natural, are being eroded, whilst we are sacrificing them for selective freedoms. Freedoms that only a few will benefit from.

These new freedoms are the freedom to say what you want to who you want without persecution. The freedom to not pay taxes and hire and fire people as you want. The freedom to employ people on zero hours contracts. The freedom to charge high rents but not maintain a house to liveable standards. These freedoms are given as to *not hold people back, because if we hold them back then no one will benefit*, when in reality the only ones that benefit are the bosses.

You are free to sell your labour, and if you freely choose not to, then you are free to die.

Our freedoms were never given to us by enlightened leaders. Weekends, severance pay, bank holidays, a limit on the working day so that you can see your family, a prohibition on child labour, retirement ages, health and safety and wage levels, these and more were advances won by the labour movements.

Furthermore, in 2019, The Sutton Trust reported that "Social mobility across the UK is low and not improving, depriving large parts of the country of opportunity. Most High ranking jobs go to privately educated children that make up less than 7% of the population."

- Britain's most powerful people are 5 times more likely to have gone to private school despite making up only 7% of the population.

- 52% of senior judges went to a private school then to an Oxbridge university.

- Politics, the media, and public service all have high percentages of privately educated people in them: 65% of senior judges, 59% of civil service permanent secretaries and 57% of the House of Lords. [25]

Furthermore, competition is also toxic for the country as a whole when it reaches certain levels. Social epidemiologists have proven a link between levels of competitiveness, social problems and income inequality. They found in countries with more income inequality (the gap between the amount the highest and the lowest earners) the more competitive people were with each other. This leads to less social cohesion and more issues such as public debt, number of violent crimes, social anxiety levels, number of prisoners, levels of drug addiction, rate of teenage pregnancy and more physical and mental health issues. The more neoliberal countries like the UK and the USA came out top. They found in countries with lower levels of income inequality that people were less hostile towards one another, more trusting, and the rates of the above health and social issues were all lower. Even little things like more people gave way when driving their car. [3]

Furthermore, we have internalised the logic of neoliberal capitalism. How many times have you felt the pressure to be productive and not lazy; or that our self-worth is reflected in our job title or the designer labels on our clothes; believing that if we work hard we will feel fulfilled and happy; or that we don't deserve to put our health or family before the needs of our job. Even much so that we take pride in our suffering and lack of time off!

This is all pure ideology and when people say these types of things to us we might disagree or even claim we believe in something else, but it is what we do, like staying on for a few hours at work unpaid or maybe we feel bad comparing ourselves to others on Instagram, it is these behaviours that matter and the thoughts that go before or after, they are the result of neoliberal capitalist ideology.

How it Started

Since the late 1970s, neoliberalism has demolished trade unions and stripped away financial regulations which has led to more wealth for people with money and a stagnation in wages for the rest of us. President Reagan imposed this in the USA and Thatcher did so in the UK. In later years, neoliberalism repurposed the function of the World Bank and the International Monetary Fund (IMF). These global institutions are in charge of overseeing cooperation in international markets, and lend money to poorer countries when they need it. With these loans comes a set of conditions which the country must adopt to get the money. These conditions are changes to the economic structure of the country and are often neo-liberal in flavour. They often stipulate that the loans cannot be spent on social programs, but that said countries should further austerity measures and the privatisation of state-owned companies including health, education and transport systems. [16]

Many Western countries have a lot of influence over the direction of the IMF and World Bank. With developing countries being the recipients of the loans, this has been called a form of *neocolonialism* in the modern age. There are currently calls to cancel the debts of many African and South American countries as they have had little benefit from these loans- in fact, they have made these countries poorer.

In 1991, in Egypt, the IMF and the World Bank put in place the *Economic Reform and Structural Adjustment Programme*. These neo-liberal reforms caused a deep social crisis in the country. This was a result of privatising public companies, and prices and rents were liberalised, causing increases. From 2005 there was unrest between the working class as many lost their jobs when the companies were sold. Later, high food prices and increasing inflation settled in, all whilst companies celebrated increased profits. The World Bank's own report showed that inequality was on the rise in a country that had 60% of the population already living in poverty. The IMF policies merged with the regimes' and they have ruined the Egyptian economy. These policies were like the ones imposed in Libya, Tunisia, India, and Syria. Neoliberalism's inability to adapt to the needs of the citizens created the environment for the Arab Spring in the early 2010's.[27]

This type of neo-colonisation is more common today as it would not be accepted by the vast majority as okay to invade countries for the resources. As we have seen with Iraq, it can be done under the cloak of delivering democracy and 'freedom'. However, it is a lot easier to do this by bending poor countries' arms with loans and reforms. China is challenging this idea and setting up its own institutions such as the Asian Infrastructure Investment Bank which the USA has not joined. Furthemore there is BRICS which includes Brazil, Russia, India, China and South Africa. This is a counter weight to the G7, a Western led economic and political group. BRICS purpose is to allow the country members to work on the basis of non-interference, and equality whilst also having mutual benefit for all. This is another chapter in the war for global hegemony.

Margaret Thatcher was more of a Marxist than most left-wingers today.

She understood that violent changes in law would change at the economic base which in turn allowed her to change society itself.

'Economics are the method: The object is to change the soul'. She also understood that a revolution involved destroying or changing your enemies. In 2002, she said her greatest achievement was "*Tony Blair and New Labour. We forced our opponents to change their minds.*"

This is how we ended up in an a-political world. A world where identity and aesthetics become the only form of politics. It was no longer viable to argue for change. The left was dead in Europe, the UK, and the USA. The neo-liberal counter-revolution was won, and we are living in its postmodern remains.

Good Neoliberalism?

Nancy Fraser, Professor of Philosophy and Politics at the New School for Social Research in New York, has since broken-down neoliberalism into ideological bite-sized chunks. She explains that following on from its initial inception, after the right lost power in the mid-1990s, neoliberalism was like an alien trying to find a host body so it would not wither out and die.

It found a host in President Bill Clinton (not the only thing he has merged with whilst in office): neoliberalism merged with progressive forces to become capitalism with a smiling face: *progressive neoliberalism*. Under this fluffy disguise, sometimes called the third-way, neoliberalism was able to fuse liberal progressive movements that were fighting for better rights, the middle classes, modernisers, the media, tech bros and monopoly capital. With the language of equality and freedom, progressive neoliberalism could please almost everyone. It promised more progress into the 21st century. This was 'the end of history'. [18]

An example of this was in the UK from 1997 to 2010, New Labour under Tony Blair paid private companies to build hospitals and schools. The private companies got contractual rights to maintain the building for the next 20-30 years, and the government would pay off the mortgage at the same time (with added interest). A government credit card otherwise known as PFI (Private Finance Initiative). Most citizens were content as they got new public facilities, governments were popular, and the private companies were making money. Furthermore, PFI allowed Britain to stay within the EU's restrictions, and Gordon Brown's, on the size of government deficits. It was kept off the books so to speak. (The EU limits state power to help centralise power to the EU centralised apparatus, hence why many refer to it as a neoliberal institution as its deficit obsession is bad economics.)

That was until the 2008 worldwide recession. Governments never directly caused the crisis, but this form of neoliberalism fed the machine. In truth, they never told the system when to stop eating. That caused it to explode. It wasn't the people who were too greedy; it was the banks and shareholders. Governments could have done something about it before, but they chose not to, believing the days of crashes were over and that the markets would regulate themselves. Eventually, government debt went through the roof because so many companies went under, and people lost their jobs. They had to resort to claiming benefits and then there was also the need to bail out banks.

Austerity, the act of cutting public spending, was put in place throughout the UK and most of Europe in response to the crash, mainly to curb the deficit to pay off the debt. The allegory of a household was used to justify these cuts however a country's economy does not work the same as your current account. This failed to boost the economy and most countries have struggled to recover since. In fact, it was a good way of justifying the further privatisation of services and cutting taxes.

Not only does it hurt public services, but compared to the USA, which invested in building and improving state infrastructure, their economy grew double the amount of the EUs after 2008. Before the crash they were equal. This obviously has effects on business, people, and industry. It was a bad move to say the least. Austerity was another excuse to cut government spending and sell off further services. [19]

These mistakes are influencing how governments react to the coronavirus pandemic. Whilst austerity may not be on anyone's lips for now, pumping loads of money into a fragile and corrupt corporate system is also a questionable idea. If anything, we saw how throwing money at private businesses during the pandemic delivered bad results. We have been left with mounds of corruption cases and a strengthened state monopoly capitalism.

Austerity left services underfunded within the framework of PFI. This framework functions as long as there is plenty of money going in, enough for private companies to take their profit out. Yet, when there is less going in, the companies still want their profit, meaning less for the services and the public. We are paying their directors bonuses. The welfare states, in both the UK and the EU, are a shell of what it was designed for, yet they have protected us during this pandemic.

∞

Over the last 50 years in most of the Western world, the image of the state as being cumbersome and inefficient has been used to spur on the privatisation of services whilst the public view it with minor threat. Under the guise of efficiency and freedom of choice, public services have been hollowed out. Services (mental health, libraries etc.) have been closed if they are not deemed effective by the government, prioritising growth over people's well-being. Yet it is forgotten that the state was instrumental in designing and inventing many things that private companies make money from today. The internet and GPS were both funded and developed by the American government. Not Google.

This economic path has also promoted the financialization of the world economy. Globalisation has gone rampant which has left individual nation states somewhat powerless to combat illegal activities and toothless international institutions scared of the private sector or in most cases working for them. Industry and manufacturing have moved abroad to poorer countries to help lower costs (and increase dividends) whilst Western countries increased their financial service industries. Not only does this affect the working class in the West but also the working class internationally. With increased manufacturing and shipping the earth is also suffering so dividends can be paid out.

In the UK, and in many countries, the working class has been demonised through television shows, newspapers, and the media. The narrative use of overarching stereotypes- that all working-class people are lazy and living off benefits- helped to justify the cutting of state help and institutions. People in lower-paid work were deemed to be worthless, as they never had a job that added to the growth of the economy. [27] Yet, it is the economy that has failed to provide secure and meaningful jobs in areas where manufacturing and other sectors have diminished, the blame for our societal flaws has been transferred to the individual. This move alone sums up the philosophy of neoliberalism. The rise of the individual at the cost of the collective.

The myth that powerful individuals and the chase of individual goals further society has been cemented in the public's psyche as common sense. It gave the impression that people are free to follow their dreams and think more individually, but it took away civil responsibility and a sense of community. Individualist hyper-meritocracy is the new societal norm.

The Diamond in the Rough

A good example of neo-liberal thinking is the film *Aladdin*. The 1992 animated film, produced by American giant Walt Disney Pictures, portrays a young down-and-out Arab boy being tricked by an evil sorcerer to obtain a magic lamp as only he can retrieve it.

In the original story, from the book *One Thousand and One Arabian Nights,* Aladdin is a lazy boy living in China. In the film, the Arabic society is portrayed as backward, and it replaces the characters of the original story with Americanised stereotypes. It forgets to mention that at one point, probably close to the time Aladdin is set, that the Arabic world was light years ahead of its European counterparts in science, mathematics, and culture. Now, you may say it is just a film, but the appropriation of an Arabic story that is changed to promote

Western ideals is in itself capitalist, and popular culture such as films or computer games can give us an insight into the dominant ideology of the time.

The view of the American dream- anyone can make it no matter what your background- is extended to even those beyond the borders of the USA. Whilst the moral of the story is like the original, there is more focus on the individual's behaviour and responsibilities. This is opposed to the original theme, which is wealth cannot make you happy, which is only passing in the retelling. It is this shift in the message that is ideological. Its over-the-top portrayal of individualism is echoed in the theme that says that every diamond, even a rough one, is unique. This deepens further the strength of personal responsibility and individualism: that the individual is sacred and above the collective. Whilst encouraging self-responsibility is a good thing, too much can make society in-cohesive; in fact thinking you are different to everyone else can hinder collective action on issues that individuals alone cannot influence, such as climate change. No doubt the people who refuse to wear masks in a global pandemic come to mind.

Another aspect of the film, common in most Disney films, is that our ultimate goal in life should be happiness. The film portrays happiness as what you must achieve at all costs, and that only you can do this. It goes on to depict freedom as a necessity to achieving happiness. Jasmine's ride on the magic carpet is symbolic here, and both the protagonist's efforts to break free from their situations furthers the narrative that freedom equals happiness. However, freedom is the ultimate illusion. This empty word has been revised so many times that if you were to ask various people what freedom means to them, they would all come up with different answers. Is freedom a black woman struggling for many years to break into journalism? Is freedom to inherit wealth, sending your children to the best private schools in the country so that they can get one of the best paying jobs in the country? How can you be free if you have to work two jobs just to keep a roof over your head? You are free to suffer whilst the rich are free from their responsibilities to society: how is that freedom?

An example of this is Jordon Peterson claiming that you can be the master of your own destiny if you make your bed in the morning and practice self discipline. Would this narrative go down so well with people who have been displaced or are starving because of a prolonged drought in Central, East, West and the Horn of Africa? Caused by climate change, these people are facing failed harvests and dying livestock which, they rely on to feed their families.

Mother Nyadang Martha, a mother from Akobo in South Sudan told Oxfam:

"All the 40 years of my life, I have never seen anything like what is happening here in Akobo. For the past four years, it is either flood, drought, famine, violence, or COVID-19. This is just too much. I am tired of living. If it continues like this, I doubt if my girls will become full adults."

Because of this drought, 13 million people have been displaced looking for water, while millions more have had to leave their homes because of conflicts. [28]

Thus, the belief that freedom equals happiness benefits the dominant ideology, and so does the narrative that anything that goes against your freedom is imposing on your right to happiness. The rhetoric of freedom is then used to justify economic freedom at the expense of people that it does not benefit, a similar use of the word is also used to justify war.

Comparing the two versions of Princess Jasmine from the animation and the recent live action film is one way of seeing how culture reflects and reinforces the dominant ideology of the day. It is also evidence of how ideologies change with the times to maintain their position.

In the animated film from the early 90s, Jasmine is a passive character that things happen to and who wants to marry for love. Whereas in the live action film from 2019, she is a strong female character who wants the law to change, not so she can marry, but so she can be Sultan. She also gets her own song and makes things happen, rather than just being a female for the male character to save. This reflects the changing roles for women in society, how, in many respects, our society has progressed when it comes to equality of the sexes. Yet, this liberal championing of the single female individual, who is a princess, also echoes the thoughts of some of our society on gender and race. Yes, we have had black CEOs, presidents, and celebrities, yet this is not evidence of no or less racism in society. Or how women in prominent places don't take away the fact there are still gendered imbalances in society. Some women can now change their company if they have the right contacts, but many others have to fight collectively to change laws that govern their own bodies, laws often made by men and the middle and upper classes.

Children who were entertained by films such as the Lion King and Toy Story have now grown up with some of the ideals of Disney. This may have positive effects such as pro-social behaviour and the morals that promote helping others, yet on the other hand the films have strengthened images of gender, racial and cultural stereotypes. Some even argue that the good-versus-evil plots of the films have led to the political polarisation that we are experiencing in our society.

So, as we can see, beyond the obvious moral messages of a piece of media, there are often underlying representations of the society that we live in. Sometimes they highlight contradictions in our system that ideology covers up, and at others they reinforce those contradictions portraying them as a natural part of the world. Here the myth that you must have complete and utter individual freedom to make it as a person is peddled, and the downside to this is 'and if you don't, it is all your fault!'.

Under progressive neoliberalism, people who were against the economic system were side-lined as archaic fossils of a by-gone era. With great rafts of the progressive centre, and right and left parts of society following this economic path, and not questioning it, there was nothing to push back. Neoliberalism, many thought, was the end of ideologies as the grand battles between capitalism and communism were over. 2008 later changed that. That is why we are so polarised. The 90s and early 2000s were so ideologically dominated by neoliberalism, anyone who challenged the norm was seen as nuts. However, real politics is back, and the people who have benefited from the system don't wanna change a thing.

The Lie That Was Told: Neoliberalism is Dying

"Progress is impossible without change, and those who cannot change their minds cannot change anything."

George Bernard Shaw, Irish playwright and philosopher

In 2019 whilst I was in quarantine I started to blog again, and I used the platform Medium. Here I quickly found many wannabe journalists, life coaches, and self-appointed gurus writing feature-length predictions about what life may be like afterwards. Our predictions never flourished post-coronavirus as we could not, and still struggle, to imagine an alternative to capitalism: instead, it all morphed into a further extension of what we already have.

The fact people saw this pandemic as a life-changing event says something, but were we, and are we, all willing and capable to change? Coronavirus could have been that change, but is humanity ready to see things differently?

Predictions throughout the pandemic sought to unleash the individual's inner good or they explored the way we could change society. From how we work out to how men interrupt in meetings on Zoom, every topic possible was and continues to be covered. Some people made predictions on a larger scale, such as how our consumption may change, whilst others talked about how you can hack the system to get rich. There are plenty of tales of how people morphed into their future selves during covid-19.

In fact, the world after coronavirus was already there by the time people had written their predictions. Designer masks, eating in greenhouses, and a fresh interest in epidemiology and medical innovations were big then. People from all over were analysing the economic and political landscapes, and how this pandemic would change the world. Many asked for a return to normality despite it not being so great before. Prior to the pandemic, we had been entering times of change after a period of relative stability in the West that lasted from the early 90s till around 2008 (often referred to as the *long 90s*). The populism of Trump was just the beginning, not the end.

Some business pundits claimed that remote working would increase; people would move to the countryside and that people prefer working remotely. Whilst that may be true for some, it is not possible for everyone. There is a clear divide between those that can work from home and those that cannot. The people that needed to leave the house to work during the pandemic had been named *the essential class*. These were (and still are) the people that keep the physical world running whilst the rest could work from the confines of their homes. In the event of a pandemic it was a necessity, but afterwards it has become a big divider. Furthermore, most of these physical jobs are not well paid or well sought after and there is often a form of health and safety risk. In fact, some of these jobs are at risk of being altered by computers but not in the way we would have imagined 20 years ago.

Instead of robots sweeping streets, we now easily imagine algorithms micro managing street cleaners. Automation and technology has been improving for decades and the coronavirus pandemic has just pushed it further and faster, but it will not replace workers how we may think. It won't be making their jobs easier, but harder. Micro-management and gamification are already a feature of work in warehouses, taxis and deliveries. Could it be coming into our homes?

Then there is artificial intelligence. It can write reports, make graphs, spreadsheets and do a number of tasks such as translation and artwork. That could be a whole book, so lets stick with the example of remote working.

Working from home will benefit many: Children can be looked after by their parents, people can cook healthier meals, they won't need to take time off work to do errands, they can spend more time with their family and work in their pyjamas. It will also benefit their mental health by cutting down on commuting and having more flexibility. This is a future many dreamed of in the 50s and 60s but sadly it will only be a reality for a select few. On the other side, people will be more disconnected from colleagues, making it more difficult to share anxieties, stresses, and concerns and take collective action or even unionise. Not to mention the people that enjoy going to work with colleagues. Also work could infiltrate our ever-shrinking private lives. That and if you can do your job from home, what is to stop your employer from hiring someone to work for much less in a different country?

Whether or not you prefer working from home, having the option is a good thing. However, there will be contradictions that need to be studied, like certain matters arising with social media, the state will be behind in regulating this activity and it will be a fresh way for large companies to exploit workers.

It also opens up the prospect of employing people outside the host country. It means that companies can shy away from their responsibilities as an employer such as paying social security, maintaining health and safety matters, and they also put the cost of working from home on to the employee. So, whilst we may save on the commute, we may lose elsewhere. The future of work post-covid was not a given paradise of working from home and going to the office when needs be. For some it has literally means bringing your work home, dissolving the space many have between the office and the sofa. As we have seen after the pandemic, it has only worked in favour for a few and the longer term effects are still to come. On a positive note, it has made the companies adapt their job offers to certain roles. Making some employees have the upper hand when negotiating contracts and conditions.

I lay out some of these pros and cons, not because I'm going off topic, but I want to use it as an example. We are not here to predict the future, and the important issue here is not the future of remote working. It is in this issue that we see the contradiction between who owns the businesses and inventions (the means of production) and what we could do with them if we had democratic control over their development and usage.

The technology is there to automate jobs and make systems more efficient. We could let more people work from home to have a better work-life balance, and not forgetting the amount of Co2 output that would be reduced. We could let systems help us work smarter so people in demanding jobs could work less but earn the same. They could plan economies to limit waste and distribute goods evenly; each according to their needs.

But we must not get away with ourselves. We cannot talk of a four-day working week, when there are nurses working 8 days a week. This is working within the hegemonic norms, something certain sections of the left struggle with. During the 2019 elections Labour faced difficult questions around their plans for a four day week, when it was pointed out there were not enough nurses to cover 5 days a week let alone 4. The struggle for a shorter working week is a good one but it has to be communicated and planned for correctly. During the same election Labour suggested free good quality broadband for the whole UK, claiming it would help business and other to be connected. The BBC labelled it 'communist broadband' and some scoffed at the idea, however when the pandemic came it suddenly became a more acceptable idea. This is hegemony changing not only because of propaganda or the 'battle of ideas' but also responding to events and the changing material conditions of people's lives.

How the French thought their country would look in the year 2000 (1910) Wiki commons

Automation and technology making life and work easier are not forgone conclusions as the cartoon *the Jetsons* would make you think. Demanding democratic control is a must if we want to improve our collective lives. So, what does this have to do with ideology. This is ideology in practice. Challenging the narrative that only Elon Musk or Jeff Bezos can call the shots regarding how technology or AI evolves, because they are great rich men and 'own' it, is pure neoliberalism. Countering it with collective proposals is what the ideological battle is about, and as we can see on the ongoing debate around remote working, there are ideological openings for the left to get a word in.

As we saw around the relaxing of the rules of the pandemic, the bosses were trying to get people back to the office as quickly as possible because the 'economy needed to function'. This included calling people lazy, saying the office culture would be missed and that we would be less productive. We have seen a synthesis of the opposing ideas of workers and bosses. Hybrid working is now a thing. People who go to the office on certain days even have a nickname: TWATS (Tuesday, Wednesday, and Thursday). This mid-way point has worked out for some. It is a compromise. This is similar to the positions of many of the workers on strike and why they were supported by a large section of the population. The problem here is these compromises, whether they be for increased wages or remote working, don't change the fundamental structure of the system. However, they do show people the limits and contradictions inherit within the system. Something we need to build upon.

20 years ago people would have laughed at the idea of a 4-day working week (for the same wages) but recently it has become a slight possibility for some workers. Are we starting to dream again? Covid has broken several of the neoliberal myths such as which workers matter. It is one of the most important, and this was reflected in the public's overwhelming support for the strikes across the UK in the summer of 2022 and further.

Another ideological common sense myth broken was the capacity of the state. During covid-19, we had half-price meals and 80% of the population's wages were covered. People worked from home and helped each other. Of course, it was a grim time but there was a fundamental shift in seeing the world differently for many. We acknowledged that the state could do things to improve our lives, but not everything has to be at the will of the markets. There were no homeless people for example! It stopped within a week.

Imagine if we were able to legislate that people have the right to work from home and that all workers that do physical labour can retire at 50, these small simple reforms would change how people see work, relate to work and balance their lives. It's here when ideology becomes important. We can begin to argue and push for more. Things can be changed, but it's the breaking of stale ideas, of what is possible and not, that becomes important here.

Making the Impossible Possible

Mark Fisher, a British cultural theorist, wrote a theory called *Capitalism Realism*. In his book of the same name, he states that capitalism realism is *"the widespread acceptance that there is no alternative to capitalism."* [29]

Capitalism realism takes on the same theory as Socialism realism. This was the art form promoted by the USSR. It did this in the form of movies, literature and art. Eventually it fell along with the Berlin wall and soviet communism was subject to a wave of anti-communist propaganda in the West. This made socialism realism look like propaganda from the outside, however its original aims were to put the workers in the centre, to replace the art of the old ruling Tsarist class.

However when we look at Western art, do we see propaganda? As art critic John Berger points out, oil painting came about not just because of the materials used, but also because of its ability to finely portray concrete objects. Many oil works from the 1500s onwards contain pictures of objects, people, land or even animals to show the wealth of the person commissioning the piece. Yet art history has been very poor at looking at why things were painted. When we consider the hundreds of paintings inside our national galleries, this was once 'propaganda' for the ruling classes of the times. This all makes socialism realism look like just another genre of painting but with workers instead of landowners.[30]

Furthermore, let us ask, what is the propaganda of OUR ruling classes today?

The movies and books we read and the advertising we see. This is why we must critique all in life, and it is why understanding ideology is key.

Ironically, as the socialist dream faded, capitalism built its own facade. It set its course with British Prime Minister, Margaret Thatcher, claiming "there is no alternative". As she did this, she carried Friedrich Hayek's book *The Road to Serfdom* in her handbag. The bible of 21st century neoliberalism. As we have already said, neoliberalism peaked in the early 2000s and then crashed with the Great Recession of 2008. We now have record levels of income inequality and increasing health and social care problems associated with this. [3]

In his book, Fisher critiques films and music that reflect the theory that he talks about. He critiques the film *Children of Men*, a dystopian film where the human race cannot have children. There are ongoing crises related to migration, war, and the economy yet in the background we still see franchise coffee shops and department stores. Capitalism is still functioning. This is where the famous phrase from the book comes in *'it is easier to imagine the end of the world, than the end of capitalism.'* a quote he took from Frederic Jameson. In a sense this means that if we imagine the end of the world, we imagine the end of capitalism or another way to put it is that we cannot imagine a world without it. Which as you can imagine is a big problem for people that want a different system. We laugh at the propaganda from the soviets, yet we are stuck in our own capitalist bubble.

Moving on, Fisher explains as part of his theory that there are tears in the fabric of the capitalist veil. Like a cloak that protects the wearer, capitalism realism seeks to protect neoliberalism from people exploring alternative ways of structuring the economy and society itself. Even believing that there could be something else would be punishable by crowds of adult centrist politicians laughing at you.

However, at points there will be tears in the facade that will allow us to see the truth of what is happening. 2008 exposed the crumbling veneer and allowed us to see that the system wasn't working as we were made to believe. Covid-19 has been similar for many and there will be more events like this in the future. This is where ideological battles become important. Not just on the TV or on social media, but in the pub, at work (if you still go to the office) and at kid's football matches. Its not enough to critique capitalism, we have to offer a viable alternative.

I still remember the footage of bankers leaving Lehman Brothers with cardboard boxes. It shocked me, not because of their job losses, but because the system had failed. If someone had told me, *"Don't worry we will build a different financial system"* I would have laughed in their face, most people would. This is the conditioning effect that neoliberalism has on us: we believe there is no alternative. I would even argue that the loss of the USSR, despite its flaws, was the biggest loss for the working class in the modern age as it has allowed the neo-liberals to argue that there are no alternatives, although China's world-beating record of pulling people out of absolute poverty is also proving this wrong.

The World Bank itself reported that *"Over the past 40 years, the number of people in China with incomes below $1.90 per day – the International Poverty Line as defined by the World Bank to track global extreme* *poverty– has fallen by close to 800 million. With this, China has contributed close to three-quarters of the global reduction in the number of people living in extreme poverty.".* No other country in the history of the world comes close to this level of development in helping improve people's lives, but we don't see it in Western media. We only see negative stories about China, which of course there are but there are also many positive ones. [31]

There has been a public appetite for change for many years, but politicians don't seem to be able to break from neoliberalism. Nancy Fraser, who coined progressive neoliberalism, described this with the story of the USA's first black president. She claims that in 2008, Barack Obama won the presidency on the language of *hope*, promising to change how the country thought about politics. Yet within months he was bailing out banks by throwing cash at them but did little to help the 10 million Americans that lost their homes. The affordable care act barely touched the sides when put in the bigger picture. He had fully embraced the progressive neo-liberal model. Obama had similar politics to Clinton before him. In 2012, he used the rhetoric of Occupy to win re-election but did little to address their goals in his second term. [18]

In the UK in 2010, a socially liberal (it claimed), refreshed Conservative Party formed a coalition government with the Liberal Democrats. This saw *reactionary neoliberalism* rise, the very sort that Obama had seen off in the States had arrived in the UK and over much of Europe. This strand of neoliberalism had different variants depending on the country, but it was pro-finance, pro-austerity, and pro-tax cuts. It claimed to stand up for the small businesses, manufacturing, and the disenfranchised middle classes, yet it cut the services they needed. Using the metaphor of comparing a nation's economy to a household, the reactionaries were able to privatise more public services and sell off the shares of the banks they bailed out to their friends.

Now it was not just the working class that were being demonised, but it was also ethnic minorities. The neo-liberal reactionaries showed their true colours with anti-immigrant, ethnocentric rhetoric and policies that made life difficult for immigrants in the country. The policy was called the hostile environment in the UK. That along with the de-funding of local councils, increasing university fees, and benefits reforms responsible for thousands of deaths. The bedroom tax, a fee that council house tenants had to pay for every extra room in their home that was not being used, is the perfect illustration of what reactionary neoliberalism is. Moreover it has enabled the far right to mobilise as it has normalised the use of anti-migrant, racist, and often sexist language.

Societies witnessed that the system was not working, and this accumulated in unrest around the world. The Occupy Movement was one of the many symptoms to appear, yet the political elites ignored it. Their blindness would cost them dearly. A political space grew in all corners of the globe. People had lost their lack of political agency under neoliberalism, as there really was not much difference between the politicians of the day. Evidence of this is in the British Labour Party's number of votes from 13.5 million in 1997 to 8.6 million in 2010. [32]

Donald Trump, Bernie Sanders, Jeremy Corbyn, Podemos, Geert Wilders, Viktor Orban, Boris Johnson, Evo Morales, Marie Le Pen, Syriza, The Five Star Movement, Matteo Salvini, and Law and Justice. Populism of the progressive and reactionary types had landed. They are not going anywhere. Populism is a strategy as opposed to an ideology. It sets out to garner support from the 'people' against an 'elite'. The people and the elite are different depending upon who is preaching to what choir. The *who* in question often has to relate to the people directly and almost always try to frame themselves as one of them. As we can see from Boris Johnson in the UK and Donald Trump, they often aren't.

The election of Donald Trump and Brexit both signalled the changing tides of the world. With decades of neoliberalism hollowing out communities, deindustrialisation, falling living standards, stagnant wages and the financialization of life, populism has plenty to get people angry about. The reactionary form of populism has had many wins, and the progressive branch not so much. In 2016, Trump and the pro-brexit campaign run on a platform of taking back control. Putting the people in charge. Neither has fulfilled this promise. But imagine what a left-wing Brexit could have been like.

Trump did give some tax cuts, bombed ISIS, pulled out of the Paris Climate Agreement, went back on Obama's positive approach to Cuba, increased military spending, and cut some labour and environment regulations. He promised to spend over a trillion dollars on infrastructure improvement, to leave NATO, to clear the country's 19-trillion dollar debt (in fact it went up to 27 trillion), and to build a wall down the border with Mexico and get them to pay for it. None of these promises came true. [33]

Populism so far has been good at whipping up a storm, but not so good at clearing up after. This is backed up by Donald Trump's failure to meet a limited number of his promises. Nancy Fraser says that instead, Trump has embraced *hyper-reactionary neoliberalism*. Ethnonationalist, anti-minorities and anti-social liberal. Trump switched his target from the economic elites of Wall Street and the Democratic party to the media, progressives, and immigrants. He failed to bring back significant manufacturing, reign in financial capital and create mass jobs as he promised.

Fraser believes that this new hegemonic bloc is unstable and just recreating the space that Trump tried to fill. She said at the time that the only thing to counter it would be progressive populism, yet the dream of this was crushed with the defeat of Bernie Sanders.[18]

In the UK, Jeremy Corbyn failed to stand up for the project of Brexit, amongst his unpopularity and four years of inter-party battles, he failed to beat the main figurehead of Brexit, Boris Johnson. With Sanders and Corbyn gone, and Joe Biden as President and Keir Starmer as Leader of the Labour Party, we see progressive neoliberalism coming back to fight off its reactionary cousin, yet we all know Trump or someone like him will be back. Rachel Reeves responsible for the financial policy of the Labour Party is already falling back into the old narrative of fiscal responsibility and all the deficit myths. Whether she is just too scared to admit it or if she believes it, this quick jump back to the economics of the Blair years shows the power of neoliberalism as a dominant ideology despite the 2008 crash and the covid-19 pandemic.

The world's economy has struggled to grow and stabilise since the 2008 crash, the ruling class know that they cannot make the same mistakes as in 2008 and they will invest. Neoliberalism has marched on like a zombie, but is it still neoliberalism if I feed it lots of money with the state being a viable player? Here is where we see the difference between the ideology of neoliberalism and the economic base of state monopoly capitalism. The ideology is used to keep the hegemonic bloc in place whilst also informing policy, practice and rhetoric. We already see Labour making a full switch back to the neoliberalism of the late Tony Blair years but this time without a charismatic leader or a growing economy.

The economy has proven during this pandemic that the market alone struggles to provide for its citizens when it needs to. The state is needed, but how the state is used is what will matter most.

Neoliberalism will adapt to the times and the material realities of society to remain the dominant ideology, even if that means the state controlling parts of the economy. But how, where and when it controls the economy is what will give us a hint of its new form. The Labour Party are already avoiding the rhetoric of nationalisation saying that they will create a British energy company. Will it compete with other companies like the NHS has to? This is keeping the sacred sheep of the markets alive. This is living within capitalism realist thought.

Even if we were able to gain back the gains of the New Deal era, they would only be slashed or sold off again at the next hint of a crisis. Or is this a turning point where we go further down the individualistic rabbit hole and revert to modern-day serfdom?

Libertarianism, the belief there should be almost no state, is also seeing a comeback. At its core, it is a more extreme version of neoliberalism. Then there is the reactionary populist right which is happy to embrace many of the ideas of neoliberalism but with little respect for public institutions or the old way of doing politics. It should be remembered that when the economy is not doing well, and privileges are threatened, the majority of self-confessed liberals and the middle classes have always sided with fascists.

That said, the way we have viewed the economy in terms of growth has come to an end if we want to continue to live on this planet. Growth sounds natural, it sounds like a good thing. The way that capitalism operates is on the basis of increasing production to gain profits, not to meet human needs or improve society. With this in mind we measure this growth with GDP (Gross Domestic Product). On average the global economy grows 3% every year, which is necessary for corporations to make a profit. This effect is exponential, meaning that if we have 3% growth every year, the global economy will double in size every 23 years, and then double itself again and again. This growth means more production, more energy, more waste and more resources every year. GDP is linked to our material footprint, which is linked to the rising of global temperatures. We cannot grow our way out of the climate crisis.[34]

Furthermore, this growth is not equal across the world, in high-income countries, we are producing more waste and using more energy. Even a full-scale change to renewable energies would mean that growth continued and by the time we got there, it would be too late. It would be like trying to catch our tail, whilst an avalanche was happening.

The rich can afford private firefighters in California like when Kim Kardashian hired them to save her home from a forest fire. The future is already here. Redistribution not growth is the answer.

The capitalist realist cloak will continue to blind us from the contradictions of our current ideology, until it has found its new form. Many say that neoliberalism is dead and economically it almost is yet the thinking and behaviour that it has created will likely get worse. When it has revived itself, we will continue as we always have done. Things might get better for a while, that is, until the next crash. Whatever happens, there will also be side effects.

The right-wing authoritarian and liberal leaning parties are in power over most of the Western world. This means minor challenges or changes to the existing economy. They will try to keep it afloat and figure out how they can use it for their own political advantage. Whilst this is happening, the left will also have to mount a challenge. But what about Latin America, China, and the Middle East, or even Russia? All of these are important.

Before 2008 there was little difference between most political parties, but progressive neoliberalism is still around today. But can it stand up to its hyper-reactionary cousin, or will we face what some have started to label post-fascism. Even if it does, it does not have the answers to today's problems. Keeping the ideology of old is not the answer. We need to smash the illusion that there is no other choice. This is not the way.

With failed progressive populism, the left, young and old, will be looking to organise and push back against whatever comes next. Maybe they will have more luck in other countries. Populism has been a rhetorical technique that has helped direct the frustrations and anxieties of both the left and right, however it is no replacement for class-based politics. The class politics of the 70's and 80's won't return in the form of miner's strikes, but it can come in other forms as we have seen. This needs to grow.

Even Joseph Stiglitz, former chief economist at the World Bank and Nobel prize winning economist, suggests that we need progressive markets that regulate capital and make the markets work for the people. He says this is the only way out of this mess. This is also supported by Thomas Piketty. He proved that in human history inequality has been continuously growing. The only times that the markets levelled out and inequality shrunk was following the two world wars when taxes on the wealthier were higher. He sees this as a flaw in the economic system and suggests that a progressive tax system and some form of socialism is needed to combat the growing levels of inequality. [2] Both of these award winning economists are liberals, just smart ones that can see that the economy of the 90s and early 2000s will not work today because the world has changed. Others struggle to fathom this and pine or the days of progressive neoliberalism.

Socialists and communists want to go further and socialise the economy, making it so that workers and citizens of the state enjoy the profits from companies rather than the corporate monopolies.

Socialism comes in many forms, and it often depends on the country and its development. What would socialism look like in Britain or Europe today? It would mean more freedom.

The pandemic has made many of us question what freedom really is. Is it freedom to work in a mask for 8 hours day in a supermarket, risking my health, just so that I can spend 50% of my wages on rent? Why should some have the freedom to flounce rules, go abroad and possibly spread the virus to me. We need to redefine freedom.

Ideology is a battle of ideas, but it is the behaviour that matters. It is the idea that influences the speech, behaviour, our approach, and policies. From my Instagram posts to government policy: they are all ideology. Every time we judge someone by neoliberal standards, we are reproducing the ideology. This obviously sounds a bit odd, and most of us millennials were born into this very ideology. It is hard to break out! But working from within ourselves, with others in our workplaces, and if you are brave enough at Christmas dinner; we can challenge this business way of thinking. This is ideology at its root. The words that leave our mouths and the things that we do with our lives. You don't need to build 'your brand' on Instagram, and you don't have to be productive. Enjoy your laziness!

We see the symbolic meaning of capitalism losing its definition in the Western world, yet without another to recognise its failings we are left with a living dead system, one in free fall that thinks it will land safely. This reminds me of the typical scene from a cartoon when the protagonist falling in the sky realises that the parachute is actually his son's school bag. But before making a 12-foot hole in the ground in the shape of his body, he hits every tree on the way down. We are currently hitting the trees with political, ecological, and health crisis after crisis.

However, unlike our animated friend, we still have not realised that we don't have a parachute and that it will be very hard to get out of any holes.

A new economic system is needed. An alternative to capitalism. Not concessions, not a deal, and not just a return back to the post-war welfare state. We need a new political economy to reduce inequality, take on climate change, and one that gives workers the profits of their labour. But most of all, an economy that doesn't put profit over people and the planet. This is socialism.

There is an alternative: we just have to find the political will to achieve it.

Author Biography

Alan McGuire is a former mental health nurse from Swindon.

He currently lives in Madrid, Spain. He is active in both the labour movement and Spanish and British politics.

He has previously had poetry published on the *Culture Matters* website and the *Sideways Poetry Magazine*. He has also written opinion articles and culture critiques for the *Huffington Post, the Local, Madrid No Frills, Naked Madrid, Mundo Obrero, Leganés Activo* and *The Morning Star.*

He is also the founder and co-host of *The Sobremesa Podcast*. A podcast that explores contemporary culture, history and politics on the Iberian peninsula.

You can contact the author via ***alanmcguire.com*** or on social media ***@amcguiri***

Acknowledgements

I would like to thank several people for their help with this book including Chloe Mansola for her edit.

I'd like to thank all my British and Irish comrades in Madrid: Eoghan Gilmartin, Matt Morgan, Tim Syme, Tim Appleton, and Leah Patten. Not forgetting my Spanish camaradas from the PCE Leganès Nucleo.

Lastly, I'd like to thank my family in both England and Spain and of course my beloved wife Laura who puts up with my ranting where I sound like a Maoist on mandy.

If you have enjoyed this book please leave a review on Goodreads and recommend it to a friend!

Bibliography

1. D. Strauss, *Global Job Losses Rise Sharply as Coronavirus Lockdowns Are Extended,* Financial Times 29/4/2020
2. T. Piketty, *Capital in the Twenty-First Century*, 2013
3. K. Pickett and R. Wilkinson, *The Spirit Level: Why More Equal Societies Almost Always Do Better,* 2009
4. Equality Trust, *The Scale of Economic Inequality in the UK* URL: https://equalitytrust.org.uk/scale-economic-inequality-uk accessed 8/5/2024
5. Jack Peat, '*British public wrong about nearly everything' poll resurfaces,* The London Economic 18/6/2022,
6. C. Berchet, J. Bijlholt, M. Ando *Socio-economic and ethnic health inequalities in COVID-19 outcomes across OECD countries,* OECD Health Working Papers No. 153. 2023
7. Zizek, The Perverts Guide to Ideology, 2012
8. P. Verhaeghe, What About Me? , 2012
9. 6: A Gramsci, Selections from the Prison Notebooks of Antonio Gramsci, 1971
10. 7: M Freeden, Ideologies and Political Theory: A Conceptual Approach, 1996
11. 8: T Eagleton, Ideology: An Introduction, 1993
12. L Althusser, On The Reproduction Of Capitalism: Ideology And Ideological State Apparatuses, 2014
13. S. Zizek, The Sublime Object of Ideology, 1989
14. T Eagleton, Culture, 2013
15. Reuters, *Greensill Capital paid David Cameron salary of over $1 million a year,* 12/7/2021
16. D Harvey, *A Brief History of Neoliberalism*, 2007
17. L. Hamourtziadou, B. Gokay, *Iraq's security 2003-2019: death and neoliberal destruction par excellence,* 2020
18. N Fraser, *The Old Is Dying and the New Cannot Be Born,*

2019

19. Jim Edward, *Austerity has measurably damaged Europe: here is the statistical evidence*, Business Insider, 29/11/2018 URL: https://www.businessinsider.com/austerity-has-damaged-europe-vs-us-gdp-growth-2018-11#:~:text=Austerity%20has%20measurably%20damaged%20E Jim%20Edwards&text=The%20Institute%20of%20International

20. *Bring Our Railway Back into Public Ownership*, We Own It, 2021 URL: https://weownit.org.uk/our-public-services/railways

21. *Britain's social mobility crisis in ten graphs*, Channel 4, 28/6/2017 URL: https://www.channel4.com/news/factcheck/britains-social-mobility-crisis-in-ten-graphs

22. J. Blanden, S. Machin, S. Rahman,. *Millennials are some of the worst hit by social mobility decline in the UK,* London School of Economics Blog. 875/2019 URL: https://blogs.lse.ac.uk/businessreview/2019/05/08/millennials-are-some-of-the-worst-hit-by-social-mobility-decline-in-the-uk/

23. History editors, *Social Darwinism*, 2018 URL: https://www.history.com/topics/early-20th-century-us/social-darwinism

24. J. Baudrillard, *Simulacra and Simulation*, 1983

25. The Sutton Trust, *Elitist Britain 2019*, URL: https://www.suttontrust.com/our-research/elitist-britain-2019/

26. L. Hamourtziadou, B. Gokay, *Iraq's security 2003-2019: death and neoliberal destruction par excellence*, Open Democracy, 2020.

27. O Jones, Chavs. The Demonization of the Working Class, 2012

28. *Climate and Food Crisis in East & West Africa*, Oxfam. 2021. URL https://www.oxfam.org/en/what-we-do/emergencies/

climate-and-food-crisis-east-and-central-africa

29. M Fisher, *Capitalist Realism – Is there no alternative?*, 2009

30. J. Berger, *Ways of Seeing,* 1972

31. *Lifting 800 Million People Out of Poverty – New Report Looks at Lessons from China's Experience,* World Bank Press Release, 2022.

32. P Kellner, *Labour's Lost Votes,* Prospect Magazine, 2012. URL https://www.prospectmagazine.co.uk/politics/50485/labours-lost-votes

33. BBC, *US election 2020: Has Trump delivered on his promises?,* 2020

34. J. Hickle, *Less is More: How Degrowth Will Save The World,* Penguin, 2020.